The Jubilee

Witness Lee

Living Stream Ministry
Anaheim, California

First Edition, May 1998.

ISBN 0-7363-0373-1

Published by

Living Stream Ministry
1853 W. Ball Road, Anaheim, CA 92804 U.S.A.
P. O. Box 2121, Anaheim, CA 92814 U.S.A.

Printed in the United States of America

98 99 00 01 02 03 / 9 8 7 6 5 4 3 2 1

CONTENTS

Title   *Page*

Preface   5

1   The Age of the Jubilee   7

2   The Possession of the Jubilee   17

3   The Freedom of the Jubilee   29

4   The Living of the Jubilee   39

PREFACE

This book is a translation of messages given by Brother Witness Lee in Chinese in Anaheim, California on August 5 through 26, 1984. The messages were not reviewed by the speaker.

CHAPTER ONE

THE AGE OF THE JUBILEE

Scripture Reading: Lev. 25:8-10, 39-41; Luke 4:16-19; 2 Cor. 6:2; Gal. 5:1; Matt. 11:28; John 8:34, 36; Acts 26:18; Rom. 8:1-2, 19-23

A GENERAL ACCOUNT OF THE TRANSLATION OF THE CHINESE BIBLE

In these messages we will consider the year of jubilee. The Chinese term for *jubilee* is not found in traditional Chinese writings; it was invented by the translators of the Chinese Bible, which is one of the best translations in the world. In the early days, some of the Western missionaries who came to China knew the Bible in its original Hebrew and Greek languages. After their arrival in China, they learned the Chinese language and desired to translate the Bible into Chinese. As they were translating the Bible, each of the missionaries would retain a top Chinese scholar as his assistant. According to their knowledge of the original languages of the Bible, the missionaries would first use spoken Chinese to express the meaning in the original languages and then ask their assistants to compose into proper writing what they had expressed in spoken Chinese. Whenever they encountered a word or phrase that did not exist in Chinese, they had to invent a new word or phrase. Many of these uniquely created terms are popularly used today and are exceptionally valuable, such as the Chinese equivalents for *Jesus, Christ, justification, redemption, sanctification,* and *jubilee.* We truly thank and praise the Lord for the newly invented vocabulary in the Chinese Bible.

Many people do not realize the difficulties encountered in translating the Bible into Chinese in the early days. Many phrases in the original languages of the Bible do not exist in Chinese. For example, certain phrases in the original text of the Bible have the meaning of *in*, such as *in God, in love, in the light, in life,* and *in Christ*. However, such expressions using *in* do not exist in Chinese phraseology. Instead, Chinese expressions use *by, through, upon,* and other such words. In Chinese, we say "walk by love" instead of "walk in love." We do not say that one person is in another. Rather, we say that one is by or through another person or that one depends upon another. Yet, *in* is a crucial word in the Bible. Therefore, the missionaries found it very difficult to translate the Bible into Chinese. Nevertheless, after much consideration, they began to adopt expressions using *in*. Thus, we can see expressions such as *in Christ* and *in love* in the Chinese Bible. Still, many times the Chinese Bible does not use *in* but *by*. In the Chinese Bible, "walk by love," for example, equals "walk in love." Nevertheless, "walk in love" has a deeper denotation. We are saved in Christ, not merely by Christ, that is, not merely by depending upon Christ. For example, when taking a steamboat, we sail on the sea not by depending upon or hanging on to the boat. We would soon lose our strength to hang on to the boat, especially if a strong wave came along. Rather, we sail on the sea by staying in the boat. In the same way, we are saved not merely by depending upon Christ but by being in Christ.

CHRIST AS OUR GOOD LAND TO BE OUR INHERITANCE

In the Chinese Bible, the term *hsi-nien* for "the year of jubilee" is a new invention. *Hsi-nien* is a good term, yet most people do not understand what it means. Since this particular term was invented during the translation of the Bible into Chinese, we need to go back to the Bible for its original meaning. In the Bible, this term is complicated. The first time it is mentioned is in Leviticus 25. At that time the children of Israel had been redeemed and delivered by God out of the land of Egypt, out of the house of bondage. Formerly, they had fallen into the land of Egypt and were serving as slaves under Pharaoh, having neither freedom nor an inheritance. This typifies that, as the descendants of Adam, we fell into the world and became captives of Satan and slaves of sin. Egypt typifies the world; Pharaoh, the king of Egypt, typifies Satan; and the children of Israel typify God's people enslaved in the world. Today people in the world have fallen into the hands of Satan to be slaves of sin. They have no freedom or rest; instead, they are toiling every day. Today not only peddlers and porters but even prominent officials and distinguished persons are toiling. Everyone is toiling; the only difference is how they toil. However, the Lord Jesus as our real Moses was sent by God to deliver us out of the land of slavery into Canaan, a land flowing with milk and honey. This good land, the land of Canaan, is Christ Himself.

Through Moses God told His people that He would bring them into a land flowing with milk and honey. Both milk and honey are produced by a combination of two kinds of lives, the animal life and the vegetable life. Milk is produced by cattle, which are of the animal life. However, milk cannot be produced by the animal life alone; it also needs the vegetable life, grass. Thus, milk is a product of the animal life nourished by the vegetable life. The principle is the same with honey. Bees are animals, but without flowers, the plant life, they would not be able to produce honey. Therefore, the phrase *milk and honey* indicates that the good land is full, not of snakes and beasts, but of cattle, bees, grass, and flowers. That the good land flows with milk and honey indicates that this land is full of the animal life and the plant life. In type, Christ is the issue of these two kinds of lives. When John the Baptist saw the Lord Jesus, he said, "Behold, the Lamb of God" (John 1:29); this speaks of the animal life. The Lord referred to Himself as a grain of wheat that died (12:24); this speaks of the plant life. He is the mingling of two kinds of lives to produce milk and honey. All this signifies that Christ as the good land is full of life, rich to the uttermost, to be our supply for our enjoyment.

God brought His redeemed people out of Egypt, through their wandering in the wilderness, into the good land of Canaan, the land flowing with milk and honey. After the children of Israel had conquered the land, God, through Joshua and the high priest, divided the good land of Canaan into twelve different portions, and each tribe was allotted a portion. The descendants of Joseph received a double portion through Manasseh and Ephraim, while the tribe of Levi received no inheritance of land. The land allotted to each tribe was not according to each one's own idea; it was altogether God's decision as to which tribe would be in the north, which tribe would be in the south, and which tribe would be in the middle. Moreover, the allotment to each tribe was according to families. Thus, each family was allotted a piece of land, and each one in the household enjoyed the inheritance of the land. Therefore, when the Israelites entered into Canaan, everyone had their own portion. There were no landlords or capitalists, and neither were there paupers, beggars, or debtors.

CHRIST AS THE YEAR OF JUBILEE, THE YEAR OF GRACE, TO FALLEN MAN

The Israelites were redeemed and blessed by God and eventually were brought into the good land of Canaan, and each family was allotted their portion of the land. Under God's care, not only were the Israelites blessed, but even their land was blessed. Every seventh year the land did not have to yield its produce. In that year the Israelites and the land were to rest. In the seventh year, no one sowed his field because this was the year ordained by God as the Sabbath year. Then after seven Sabbath years, there was the Pentecostal year, the fiftieth year. The Pentecostal year was not just a Sabbath year; it was beyond human description. Because of this, the translators of the Chinese Bible struggled to invent the Chinese term *hsi-nien,* the year of jubilee, to describe it. After the Israelites entered the land of Canaan, every fiftieth year was a year of jubilee to them. Fifty years signifies the entire course of fallen human life. The year of jubilee, which is the fiftieth year, signifies the conclusion of our fallen human life.

As we have seen, the Israelites were redeemed by God; they left Egypt, journeyed through the wilderness, and entered into Canaan. After entering into the land of Canaan, each family received a portion of the good land flowing with milk and honey for their rich enjoyment. However, some of the people were lazy and gluttonous. Lazy people like to eat, but they do not like to work. To be sure, one who is lazy and gluttonous becomes poor. In ancient times the people did not have much to sell, so when they became poor, they sold their land. However, if the land had been sold permanently, in just a few generations there would have been an extreme disparity between the rich and the poor. Therefore, God told the Israelites, "The land shall not be sold into permanent ownership, for the land is Mine; for you are aliens and sojourners with Me" (Lev. 25:23). They were not to sell their portion of land, the possession that they had received from God, into permanent ownership. This is unlike the sale of land today, in which once land is sold, it is sold forever. The longest duration for which a piece of land could be sold was fifty years. After a man sold his land, in the fiftieth year, the year of jubilee, he as the original owner would receive back his land.

Furthermore, some of the people were so gluttonous and lazy that even after selling their land they were still in poverty, and they had no alternative but to sell themselves as slaves. Nevertheless, when the year of jubilee arrived, they no longer remained slaves but obtained their release. In the year of jubilee, which the Israelites were to sanctify, they proclaimed release throughout the land to all its inhabitants, and each one returned to his possession and to his family (Lev. 25:9-10). No one needed to pay for redemption; everyone freely recovered his possession and his freedom. Therefore, in the fiftieth year, no one was without land and no one was in slavery. Therefore, the year of jubilee was a grace to them.

Isaiah 61:2 calls the year of jubilee "the acceptable year of Jehovah." This can also be translated, "the year of Jehovah's grace." This verse is included in the Scripture which the Lord Jesus read in Luke 4:17-19, where the above phrase reads, "the acceptable year of the Lord, the year of jubilee." In Isaiah it is the year of grace, whereas in the New Testament it is the year of jubilee. Therefore, the year of jubilee is the year of grace. Man became a vile sinner, not only lazy and gluttonous but also reckless and lawless. Laziness and gluttony made him so poor that he had to sell his possession, and recklessness and lawlessness caused him to become so destitute that he had to sell himself. Consequently, he fell into a situation in which he had neither his possession nor his freedom. However, in the year of jubilee every owner is returned to what he has sold, and everyone regains his freedom.

Politicians and philosophers have been trying their best to find ways to meet the needs of people, but the more "isms" they invent, the more people suffer. What the Bible teaches is far better than any theory or "ism." What we need is not a theory or an "ism" but the coming of the Lord Jesus into mankind. In His coming He was anointed by Jehovah to announce the gospel to the poor, and He was sent to proclaim release to the captives and recovery of sight to the blind, to send away in release those who are oppressed, and to proclaim the year of God's acceptance of man, the year of jubilee, which is the year of grace. The year of jubilee is the time when God forgives and accepts man.

As a type in the Old Testament, the year of jubilee is recorded in Leviticus 25, and as a prophecy it is found in Isaiah 61. The type was given about fifteen hundred years before the coming of the Lord Jesus, and the prophecy was given about seven hundred years before His coming. During this time, however, the Jews were altogether ignorant of the significance of the year of jubilee in Leviticus 25 and the year of grace in Isaiah 61. Over the years, they simply kept the regulations of the law according to their tradition, worshipping on every Sabbath day and going to the synagogues to listen to teaching. But one day the Lord Jesus came, and on a particular Sabbath day He entered the synagogue, picked up the scroll, and opened it to Isaiah 61, which prophesies that God would anoint the Lord Jesus with His Spirit to announce the gospel to the poor and to proclaim the acceptable year of the Lord, the year of jubilee. Then Jesus said, "Today this Scripture has been fulfilled in your hearing" (Luke 4:21). The Jews bore witness to Him and marveled at the words of grace proceeding out of His mouth (v. 22). However, to this day they still do not understand the true meaning of these words of grace.

Today we understand the true significance of the words of grace spoken by the Lord. God created man with the purpose that man would be a vessel to contain Him for His expression. Hence, immediately after man was created, God gave Himself to man to be man's possession. The inheritance that God has given to us is God Himself. He has not given us anything other than Himself because, in God's view, everything else is dung. The inheritance spoken of in the Bible is the inheritance among the saints to be received by all those who believe into the Lord (Acts 26:18). This is God Himself. We are those who inherit God. Therefore, after God created Adam, He did not say much to him; He simply indicated that He wanted Adam to receive Him to be his real possession. However, due to his fall, man forsook God, lost God as his possession, and fell into the world. Consequently, man sold not only his own possession but also himself.

When considering human society, we may divide human beings into three categories: optimists, pessimists, and those in between. Many optimists are dreamers and persons without sobriety, and they are filled with imaginations about everything. In the eyes of pessimists, however, nothing is good. To them, China is not good, and America is also not good. When they are in one place, they say another place is better, and when they are in the other place, they say that the first one was better after all. Those in between are neither overly optimistic nor overly pessimistic; they are very clear-headed. They teach their children to study hard, to endeavor, to be sure to graduate from college, and to pass the English language test so they can go to the United States to study. If they do not obtain a Ph.D., at least they receive a master's degree. Then after getting their degree, they work even harder so they can get married, have a family, and build up a career. However, regardless of whether they are optimists, pessimists, or in between, they have all lost God as their possession and have sold themselves to be slaves of Satan.

Ephesians 2:12 says that people living in the world today have no hope and are without God. Whether rich or poor, noble or base, civilized or barbaric, everyone is the same; all have no hope and are without God. Not only so, people today have fallen to such an extent that they have sold themselves to sin and Satan. Some people have sold themselves to sinful things, such as extravagant eating and drinking, sexual indulgence, gambling, and drug addiction. With others it may not be as obvious; nevertheless, they also have sold themselves and are therefore without freedom, having no control over their own will. Those who are unmarried think that marriage is the way to be freed from problems. After marriage, however, they discover that instead of obtaining freedom they have entered a new kind of slavery. The basic problem is that man has sold himself and lost God; thus, he has completely lost his freedom and his own possession and has become a slave. Paul says in Romans 7:14, "But I am fleshy, sold under sin." Not only the unbelievers, but even many who are believers are still not wholly delivered from the slavery under Pharaoh.

Therefore, in the year of jubilee there are two main blessings: the returning of every man to his lost possession and the liberation from slavery. If we want to be truly free and able to enjoy God as our possession, we must receive the Lord Jesus as the real jubilee in us. If we have Him, our possession is recovered and our freedom is returned to us. The Lord Jesus has released us that we may have God as our possession and be delivered from the bondage of sin and Satan so that we may have real freedom. Every one of us who has experienced the grace of the Lord can testify that before we were saved, we had no freedom and no control over ourselves. Now that we have been saved, the Lord has released us from within so that we are no longer slaves. Not only so, we have been brought back to God as our possession. The Lord Jesus said in Matthew 11:28, "Come to Me all who toil and are burdened, and I will give you rest." We are no longer those who toil and are heavily burdened; we are those who have freedom and enjoy rest. Furthermore, we are no longer poor; instead, we have God as our inheritance (Acts 26:18; Eph. 1:14; Col. 1:12). This is the meaning of the year of jubilee.

EVERYTHING BEING TO OUR SATISFACTION

The Lord told Paul, "I send you, to open their eyes, to turn them from darkness to light and from the authority of Satan to God, that they may receive forgiveness of sins and an inheritance among those who have been sanctified by faith in Me" (Acts 26:17b-18). As we have seen, the inheritance referred to in this verse is God Himself. In 2 Corinthians 6:2, Paul says, "Behold, now is the well-acceptable time; behold, now is the day of salvation." Paul exhorts us to receive the Lord right away because now is the acceptable year of the Lord, the year of jubilee. The year of jubilee is a holy year, a year of grace. If we have jubilee, we have God; if we have God, we have grace.

The Chinese word for *jubilee* means *everything being to one's satisfaction*. When everything is to our satisfaction, we are in the jubilee. *Jubilee* means having no worry or anxiety, no concern or care, no lack or shortage, no sickness or calamity, and no problems whatsoever, but rather having all benefits; hence, everything is to our satisfaction. How is it possible today for a person to have everything to his satisfaction? Every day nothing in our human life is to the satisfaction of our heart's desire. Perhaps things are satisfactory today, but tomorrow they may not be. Therefore, our human life is not always satisfying, and our environment is not always gratifying. Everything can be satisfying to us only after we have gained the all-inclusive Christ as our enjoyment. In Philippians 4, Paul indicates that he knew Christ and experienced Him to such an extent that everything was to his satisfaction. He says, "I have learned, in whatever circumstances I am, to be content. I know also how to be abased, and I know how to abound; in everything and in all things I have learned the secret both to be filled and to hunger, both to abound and to lack. I am able to do all things in Him who empowers me" (vv. 11b-13). It is not outward persons, matters, or things but Christ within who enables us to be calm and free of worries as we face all kinds of situations.

In the age of the Old Testament, which was the age of law before the coming of Christ, man was in the position of a slave. It was not until Christ came that He proclaimed the coming of the year of jubilee (Luke 4:16-21). It is easy to understand the year of jubilee as lasting only for a year. However, the word *year* implies an age. We may say that "the year of jubilee" refers to the age of the jubilee, not just to one year, the fiftieth year. The fiftieth year typifies an age, an era. Dispensationally, the age of jubilee is divided into two periods. One period is the New Testament age, which is the age of grace today; the other period is the age of the millennium, which is the fullness of the jubilee.

According to the dispensation, Christ has already come, so the age of jubilee is here, but we do not have the jubilee in us unless we have allowed the Lord Jesus to come into us. Thus, according to experience, Christ must come into us to be our jubilee. Not only so, even if we have believed into Christ and have allowed Him to come into us, unless we allow Him to live in us and unless we live by Him, we are not practically living in the jubilee. If we live by Christ in a certain matter and allow Him to live in us, we enjoy jubilee in that matter. In this way everything pertaining to that particular matter is to our satisfaction. In our married life, for example, if we allow Christ to live in us and we also live by Christ, then everything in our marriage will be to our satisfaction. Whatever is unpleasant becomes pleasant, and whatever is not satisfying becomes satisfying. The same is true in going to school, in teaching school, and in doing business. If we allow Christ to live in us and if we live by Him, everything is to our satisfaction. Otherwise, everything is a problem, and nothing is a jubilee. In other words, when Christ comes into us, jubilee comes into us. Do not think that just because we are saved, we have the jubilee. Christ is our jubilee whenever we live by Him, but He is not our jubilee when we do not live by Him.

The year of jubilee is Christ; therefore, the year of jubilee is the year of grace, because grace is God Himself in Christ to be our enjoyment. When we hear the gospel, we hear the jubilee. Once we repent and believe into the Lord, jubilee enters into us. From then on, at any time and in any matter, in dealing with anyone or anything, if we live by Christ, Christ is our jubilee. Sometimes we may have the painful experience of putting Christ aside and thus losing God temporarily. Once we have lost God, we have sold ourselves and become slaves again. However, once we begin anew to enjoy the Lord Jesus, we have God and we enjoy freedom. At this time, within us everything is to our heart's satisfaction, and the jubilee is in us. We are happy and rejoicing, we prosper, and we live long. This is the meaning of the jubilee.

CHAPTER TWO

THE POSSESSION OF THE JUBILEE

Scripture Reading: Lev: 25:9-13; Psa. 16:5, 2; 90:1; Acts 26:18; Eph. 1:14; Col. 1:12; Eph. 2:12; Luke 15:11-24

In the previous message we have seen something concerning the age of the jubilee. The jubilee refers not only to a day or a year but to an entire period of time. In typology the jubilee lasted a year, but in fulfillment it refers to the entire New Testament age and the millennium. To God's chosen people, the entire New Testament age is the age of the jubilee. In this message, we will consider another crucial point, the possession of the jubilee.

THE SITUATION OF FALLEN MAN

The Bible calls the fiftieth year among the Israelites the year of jubilee. In that year every owner was returned to his lost possession, and everyone who had sold himself as a slave regained his freedom. Exodus 1 shows us that when God's elect, the Israelites, fell into Egypt, they not only lost their possession but were afflicted and enslaved by Pharaoh, king of Egypt. This is a picture depicting the condition of fallen man. A person living on the earth has two things: himself and his possessions. Whatever a person has can be put into one of these two categories. We all have ourselves; in this respect we are all equal. With regard to our possessions, however, we are not equal; some may have houses, lands, stocks, bank accounts, a wife, children, and grandchildren as their possessions. However, fallen man has lost everything and even sold himself as a slave.

The children of Israel fell from the good land into Egypt, the land of slavery, and eventually they lost everything. The land of Canaan that God had given to them was no longer theirs. It was not that the land left them but that they left the land. They left their possession, the good land of Canaan, and brought everything with them into Egypt. After losing the good land, they lost themselves; they had no freedom and became Pharaoh's slaves. This is the fullest type in the Bible depicting fallen mankind. According to this picture, as fallen mankind we have lost our possession, and we have also sold ourselves, becoming slaves who own nothing. This was the situation of the children of Israel in the land of Egypt, and it is also the situation of the entire human race.

THE JUBILEE BEING AN AGE OF ECSTASY FOR OUR SALVATION

In the previous message, we defined the Chinese term for *jubilee* as *everything being to our satisfaction.* In the jubilee, all things are pleasant and satisfying to our heart, and we are free from anxiety, at ease, excited, and exultant. In English, the word *jubilee* denotes a rejoicing, a joyful shouting. The Hebrew word for *jubilee* is *yobel,* which means a joyful noise, a shouting with the blasting of a trumpet, and a proclamation. It is a proclamation not of sorrow or lamentation but of the gospel, the good news of great joy.

When the children of Israel, God's chosen people, fell into a pitiful situation, God came to redeem them through Moses out of the land of Egypt that they might gain their freedom. When God led them out of Egypt, He performed a great miracle by separating the waters of the sea for them to pass through. Then, when they crossed the Red Sea and saw their enemies drowned and buried, they were in ecstasy, shouting and dancing for joy. Miriam led them to sing with great jubilation on the bank of the Red Sea. Fighting was the men's job, whereas singing was the women's specialty. We should be women in this way before God, and the more excited we are, the better. We should not remain in oldness, embracing the traditional way of Christianity, the way of having a Sunday morning service in a rigid manner. Instead, we should exult, as Psalm 100:1 says: "Make a joyful noise to Jehovah, all the earth." In Hebrew, *make a joyful noise* means to shout together noisily to

Jehovah. However, the Chinese translators dared not translate it in this way and therefore rendered it as "shout for joy
unto the Lord." Ezra is another book in the Bible that has a
record of people making a joyful noise. When the foundation of
the temple was laid, after the children of Israel had returned
to Jerusalem from their captivity, all the people shouted with
a loud shout. They could not discern the sound of the shout of
joy from the sound of weeping, for the people shouted with a
loud shout (3:11-13). Some may ask, "Doesn't 1 Corinthians
14:40 say that in the meetings all things should be done
becomingly and in order?" This is true, but the Bible has not
only 1 Corinthians 14 but also the Psalms. There are many
verses in the Psalms that tell us to make a joyful noise and to
rejoice, and not only to rejoice but also to exult and leap for joy.
When the jubilee came, millions of Israelites made a joyful
noise in a loud and spontaneous way, shouting with joy, even
at the same time. Today choirs are orderly because they sing
in a rigid way, without any jubilation, but if we all sing with
excitement, it is hard to be altogether orderly.

The jubilee is an age of ecstasy. The New Testament age is
an age of ecstasy, and a Christian is a person in ecstasy. Over
fifty years ago, Brother Nee said, "If, as a Christian, you have
never reached the point of being beside yourself, you are not
up to the standard." He added that we should be beside ourselves before God but soberminded before men. Some seize
this word and say, "See, didn't Brother Nee say that we
should be soberminded?" Yes, we need to be soberminded
before men, but have we ever been beside ourselves before
God? The Bible has many sides; we cannot look only at one
side. Yes, we should be soberminded before men, but to be
soberminded does not necessarily mean to be quiet. To shout
in the meetings is not to be deranged and to yell in a frenzied
way. We may shout for joy and still be soberminded. On the
one hand, we rejoice and make a joyful noise, but on the other
hand, we are soberminded, exercising restraint. If we, as
Christians, have never reached a point of being beside ourselves or being "crazy," if we have never been in ecstasy
before God, we are not up to the standard. Rather, this shows
that we do not have a sufficient enjoyment of God. If we have

a sufficient enjoyment of God, we will leap for joy. Even as an old man I am often beside myself before God, yet those around me may not be aware of it. It seems that I am serious every day, coming and going according to a prescribed schedule, yet God knows the real condition. We have a real reason to be beside ourselves. If there is no joy in us, we cannot be beside ourselves, but if we are always enjoying God, we will reach a point where we cannot help but be beside ourselves. In the same way, because the children of Israel enjoyed the grace of God's all-sufficient redemption, when they crossed the Red Sea, they shouted and leaped for joy, praising and singing with a loud voice, and cheering unceasingly.

After this, God brought them through the wilderness into Canaan and allotted the good land of Canaan to them. Each tribe received an allotment of land, and each family within each tribe also received an allotment. Furthermore, each household within each family enjoyed their portion of the allotment. Therefore, once they entered Canaan, everyone possessed a portion of land. There were no rich ones or poor ones because all the households were equal, each possessing a portion of land. There was no need for anyone to become a slave because everyone was his own landlord. There were no small landlords or big landlords; they were all the owners of their own land. Moreover, they lived a wealthy life because the land was a land flowing with milk and honey.

However, after receiving their allotted portions of the land, some of them slowly declined and became lazy. Some who were gluttonous and slothful gradually became poor. They began to sell what they owned, and even after selling their land, they eventually had to sell themselves as slaves. God, who is wise, foreknew all these things, so He set up a simple ordinance. In the forty-ninth year after the children of Israel entered Canaan, the trumpet was to be blown on the tenth day of the seventh month throughout all the land. The tenth day of the seventh month was the day of propitiation. Based on the propitiation of sins, freedom was proclaimed to all the people of Israel. Therefore, if someone had sold his land, he would be returned to his land, and if someone had sold himself as a slave, he would regain his freedom. There may have been many who had sold their land and themselves. Those who had lost their possession and had become slaves must have danced and been in ecstasy when they heard the blast of the horn, the silver trumpet, proclaiming the jubilee. This shows the significance of the jubilee. God's wisdom is immense and incredible. At the arrival of the fiftieth year, there was no more selling of land or of persons; every household had a portion of land once more. Every fifty years there was a balance of the ownership of the land; this was the fairest way to deal with the land.

IN REDEMPTION GOD BEING OUR POSSESSION FOR OUR ENJOYMENT

We must now consider what man's possession is. Psalm 16:5 says, "Jehovah is the portion of My inheritance and of My cup; / You maintain My lot." An inheritance is a possession. The land is not our real possession; rather, God is our possession. The land is merely a type, a symbol, and a figure. How can we say that God is man's possession? From Genesis 1:26 and Romans 9:21-23 we can see clearly that man was created by God to be His vessel. A vessel as a container is empty by itself; hence, it needs content. The content of a vessel is its possession. An empty cup is a destitute cup. One who is thirsty desires a drink, but an empty cup cannot quench his thirst. To be empty is to be poor, and to be poor is to be empty. Man is a vessel of God; hence if man does not have God, he is empty and poor. The first chorus of *Hymns,* #1080 says, "Vanity! Vanity! / Vanity! Vanity! / 'Tis chasing the wind, / It's all vanity!" The last chorus says, "Christ without, all is vain! / Christ within, all is gain! / All things are vain, / Christ only is gain!" Man without Christ is vain. Hence, man's real possession is not land or a house, and neither is it a wife or children; man's possession is God. God created man as His vessel to contain Him. If we as a vessel do not have God as our content, we are empty and poor.

After God created Adam, He put Adam in front of the tree of life, indicating that He wanted Adam to receive the tree of life; besides this, He indicated little else to Adam. What is the tree of life? The tree of life is God. The Lord Jesus said, "I am the bread of life; he who comes to Me shall by no means hunger, and he who believes into Me shall by no means ever thirst" (John 6:35). Psalm 36:9 also says, "For with You is the fountain of life." The Lord is the tree of life and the river of life; he who believes into Him eats and drinks Him and is satisfied. To be sure, God is our possession. Furthermore, according to Psalm 16:5 God is not only our inheritance, but also the portion of our cup. In this verse, *inheritance* is a general expression, whereas *cup* is a more personal expression. God is not only our inheritance but also the portion of our cup for our enjoyment. God is not only our possession but also our real enjoyment. Moreover, God maintains our allotted portion.

God presented the tree of life to Adam, but Adam did not take it; hence, he lost his portion of the enjoyment of God. Adam fell from God's presence, and as a result, all the people of the world lost God. Therefore, Ephesians 2:12 says that people living in the world today have no hope and are without God. The prodigal son in Luke 15:11-32 is a portrait of all mankind. From kings and presidents to street sweepers and beggars, everyone is a prodigal son who has become penniless and who lives with "hogs." The fall of man is a fall from God, a fall from man's possession. Man has lost God as his possession and enjoyment. This is the first step of man's loss.

The second step is that in the fall, man sold himself to sin. Paul says in Romans 7:14, "I am fleshy, sold under sin." As fallen sinners, we have lost God, and we are without God. Not only so, we have sold our members to sin to become slaves of sin (6:19). Sin dominates man. Today people in the world, no matter who they are, are under the domination of sin. Some people have a higher degree of intellect and thus are controlled by their reason. For the sake of society, their relatives, and their friends, they are not reckless outwardly, but they are still reckless in their mind. Who is not sold to sin in his heart? We have all sold ourselves to sin.

God called Paul and said to him, "I send you, to open their eyes, to turn them from darkness to light and from the authority of Satan to God, that they may receive forgiveness of sins and an inheritance among those who have been sanctified by faith in Me" (Acts 26:17b-18). This inheritance is God as our possession, that is, God as our land with its rich produce. Today man needs land to provide food for his living and a lodging for his rest. As we have seen, Psalm 16:5 says, "Jehovah is the portion of My inheritance," and Psalm 90:1 says, "O Lord, You have been our dwelling place / In all generations." *Hymns,* #600 is written based on these two psalms. The general idea of the hymn is that God is our eternal portion, our everlasting all, and our safe abode. God is our land and our dwelling place. It is no wonder that when the Lord Jesus came, He said, "Come to Me all who toil and are burdened, and I will give you rest" (Matt. 11:28). Moreover, in John 15:4 He said, "Abide in Me." Today all men have lost God as their possession, and they have no real dwelling place. Fallen people are all drifting about and wandering without a home. Although they may live in high-rise buildings or large mansions, within them there is no rest, no dwelling place. Man is wandering because he has lost God. God is man's real dwelling place and real possession.

THE PREACHING OF THE GOSPEL BEING THE PROCLAMATION OF GOD'S JUBILEE, THAT MAN MAY BE SAVED AND RETURNED TO HIS POSSESSION TO ENJOY GOD

When we preach the gospel, we proclaim God's jubilee to others. In Luke 4:18-19 the Lord Jesus made a proclamation concerning the coming of the jubilee. The proclamation of the jubilee in Luke 4 governs the central thought of the whole Gospel of Luke, and the parable of the prodigal son in Luke 15 is an excellent illustration of the jubilee. Before examining this parable, however, we must consider a few verses. In Ephesians 1:13-14, Paul says, "In whom you also, having heard the word of the truth, the gospel of your salvation, in Him also believing, you were sealed with the Holy Spirit of the promise, who is the pledge of our inheritance unto the redemption of the acquired possession, to the praise of His glory." What does it mean to be saved? To be saved is to return to our inheritance, to return to God, to come back to God and enjoy Him anew as our possession. God is our inheritance, and after we are saved, the Spirit of God is in us as the pledge, the guarantee, the proof, and the security of our inheritance. In Greek, the word for *pledge* or *guarantee* also means *sample.*

A sample is a foretaste, guaranteeing the full taste in the future. Today the Holy Spirit is in us as the guarantee, the sample, of God as our enjoyment, giving us a foretaste and guaranteeing our full enjoyment of God in the future. Therefore, to be saved is to gain God. We have not only obtained salvation, but even more we have obtained God. When we have God, we have everything; without God, we have nothing. We are saved only when we have God, and with God we have everything. Therefore, God is our inheritance.

Furthermore, Colossians 1:12 says, "Giving thanks to the Father, who has qualified you for a share of the allotted portion of the saints in the light." Today God has become our blessed portion in Christ. Apart from Christ, people live in the world, having no hope and being without God. Outside of Christ, we are without God in the world. We, however, can no longer say that we are apart from Christ. We are in Christ, and we have God. This is not merely a saying but a reality. Perhaps some may ask, "Why is it, then, that some Christians are still unhappy?" We may illustrate this with electric lights. Lights may be installed in a building, and the electricity may be connected, but if we do not use the switch to turn them on, the lights do not shine. There is electricity, but there are no lights; practically, this is the same as having no electricity. This is the situation of many Christians. Even though they have God, they are like lights that do not shine because they do not "turn on the switch" by taking God as their portion.

As Paul says in Ephesians 2:12, we were apart from Christ, having no hope and without God in the world. Today, however, we are no longer apart from Christ. Rather, we are in Christ. We have God, and we "turn on the switch" to enjoy God as our possession. The jubilee is altogether related to our possession, and our possession is God. When we have God, we have the jubilee; when we have God, everything is to our satisfaction. Our preaching of the gospel is our blowing of the trumpet of redemption to proclaim to the world, "Behold, now is the well-acceptable time; behold, now is the day of salvation," the year of jubilee (2 Cor. 6:2). Though man has fallen far from God, God is waiting for him, longing for his return.

We may now consider the parable of the prodigal son in Luke 15:11-32. We are all very familiar with the parable of the prodigal son's return. Some have even known this story from their childhood. In this story, the Lord Jesus speaks of a certain father who had two sons. The younger one, being befuddled, asked the father to give him his share of the inheritance. After he received his inheritance, he went out and lived dissolutely until he spent it all. Then he had no choice but to go and join himself to a citizen of a "distant country," which signifies the satanic world. This citizen, who may be compared to Satan, was more oppressive than Pharaoh and sent him to feed the hogs. Pharaoh sent the people to build cities, but in this parable a citizen sent the son to feed hogs, which is worse. Building cities is a matter of sweating and making bricks, but in order to feed hogs, one has to associate with them. Eventually, the son desired to eat the carob pods which the hogs ate, yet even then his hunger was not satisfied. As a result, the prodigal son came to his senses and returned to his father's house.

A Chinese proverb says, "The return of a prodigal son is more precious than gold." Many people refer to this parable when they preach the gospel. However, this parable is mainly concerned not with the prodigal son's return but with the father who looks for his son and accepts him with embraces and affectionate kisses. The father's acceptance of the son was the "year of jubilee" to him. A father's great fear is that his children might run away from home; this is a very painful thing. Although it is painful for an only son to run away from home, we may think that a father of many children would not care as much about one son. However, a father treasures every one of his children. A father even cannot bear it when a son runs out of the house for a short time. In this parable, the father not only looked occasionally for his son, but he must have stood at the door of his house every day, eagerly waiting for his son's return. Therefore, when the son returned, the father saw him from afar and immediately ran to him to embrace him and kiss him (v. 20). This was his acceptance of the son. The day of the return of the prodigal son was a year of jubilee to him. That was the year of grace, the acceptable year of God. God accepts all fallen and repentant prodigal sons.

According to spiritual significance, this story depicts a fallen man who completely lost his possession in the house of God the Father. He left his own possession and sold himself as a slave. Today, all fallen people, regardless of their profession, whether presidents, kings, or poor beggars, are "feeding hogs." To feed hogs is to engage in unclean business. We may say that a profession in politics is dark, but in reality which profession is not dark? If politics is the darkest profession, then commerce is the second darkest, but is education not dark? Those who have a Ph.D., medical doctors, and everyone else are also in darkness. Everyone is "feeding hogs." The most obvious result of feeding hogs is to become unclean; this indicates one's engagement in unclean things. In today's society, which profession does not practice giving and receiving bribes? If one does not give bribes, he has no way to succeed. Whose money is earned in an absolutely clean manner? It is no wonder the Lord Jesus gives money a name, "the mammon of unrighteousness" (Luke 16:9). The very nature of money is unrighteous. Even if a person seems to be righteous, as long as he makes money and acquires a fortune, he is "feeding hogs"; he is engaged in unclean business. Perhaps when some hear this, they may say, "Since this is the case, from now on I will give up my schooling and abandon my job." This is not what we mean. In this world people have to work lest they become vagrants and loafers. How can one eat without working? Rather, this story is a picture showing us that once a fallen man leaves God, he goes to "feed hogs," regardless of what profession he is in. We should consider seriously whether we are clean in our work. All fallen people working in society are "wallowing in a pigpen," although some eat better "carob pods" than others. Everyone is "feeding hogs" and eating "carob pods."

When the prodigal son considered his situation, he may have asked himself, "Why am I doing this? My father is very rich, so why should I perish here in famine?" This is a sinner's repentance. However, the concept of a sinner after his repentance is to return home to work. Therefore, the prodigal son went on to say, "I will rise up and go to my father, and I will say to him, Father, I have sinned against heaven and before you. I am no longer worthy to be called your son; make me like one of your hired servants" (vv. 18-19). Then he rose up and went to his father to speak according to what he had prepared. However, the father did not want to hear what he had to say, so before the son could finish his speaking, the father interrupted him and told the servants, "Bring out quickly the best robe and put it on him, and put a ring on his hand and sandals on his feet. And bring the fattened calf; slaughter it, and let us eat and be merry" (vv. 22-23). The fattened calf signifies Christ, who is God. God in Christ has become the fattened calf for the enjoyment of the repentant and returning prodigal sons. To us, this is the jubilee.

Therefore, Luke 15:11-32 is an illustration of the jubilee proclaimed in Luke 4:18-19. The prodigal son sold his possession and himself. One day he returned to his possession and his father's house. That was a jubilee, a liberation, and everything became pleasant and satisfying. In the father's house there was only enjoyment with eating and drinking; there was no labor. This corresponds to Leviticus 25:11, which says that the people were neither to sow or reap in the year of the jubilee; they should only eat and enjoy. Furthermore, they could only eat of the produce directly from the field. This means that they ate what God supplied without the need of their own labor. Similarly, the father in Luke 15 did not listen to what the son had to say about being a hired servant. Instead, the father desired to give the son the fattened calf for him to eat and enjoy. No one is unworthy; rather, all are worthy because God says, "I have accepted you." The jubilee is the age, the time, of God's acceptance, indicated by the father's acceptance of the prodigal son in Luke 15.

The jubilee in the Bible is the age of the gospel, which is this age. Once we repent and turn to God by receiving the Lord Jesus, we obtain God within. This is the beginning of our jubilee. From that day onwards, our whole life is a jubilee, and we enjoy the jubilee forever. We can continually enjoy God as our possession. We thank and praise the Lord that our jubilee will be richer and richer from now unto eternity. This is the meaning of the possession of the jubilee.

CHAPTER THREE

THE FREEDOM OF THE JUBILEE

Scripture Reading: Lev. 25:39-41, 54; Luke 4:18-19; Acts 26:18; John 8:34, 36; Rom. 7:14; 6:6-7; 8:2; Gal. 5:1

ENJOYING GOD AS THE POSSESSION OF THE JUBILEE AND OBTAINING THE FREEDOM OF THE JUBILEE

In the preceding chapter we saw the possession of the jubilee, and in this message we shall see the freedom of the jubilee. Possession and freedom are both positive, but there is a difference between them. Some may say that they would rather have freedom than a possession, but this concept is not correct. Our possession is God. We cannot renounce God, saying that we want freedom instead of God, because without God there is no freedom. Our possession is God, and our freedom comes from our enjoyment of God. When we have our possession and enjoy our possession, the result is that we have freedom. Freedom is to be without oppression or deficiency. Some people apparently are not oppressed, but they are poor. Only those who have suffered the misery of poverty really know what poverty is. Poverty is a tremendous bondage. Nothing oppresses people more than poverty; it can oppress people to the extent that they have no escape. How we thank God that today He is our possession, and when we enjoy Him, we have freedom!

Without the types of the Old Testament, we would have no way to understand the plain words of the New Testament. Thus, the Old Testament types are very precious to us. Kindergarten students can appreciate pictures and models. If we speak about an airplane, they may not understand what an airplane is, but if we show them a picture or a model of an

airplane, they will immediately understand. The Bible seems
to use the "kindergarten teaching method": the New Testament contains plain words, and the Old Testament contains
pictures. The New Testament clearly tells us that without
God, we lose our possession; that is, we do not enjoy God, and
consequently we sell ourselves into slavery. We have lost God
and have been sold into sin. However, if the Bible only says
this without giving us a picture, we would still not be clear.
This is why the Old Testament types are helpful. Each point
in the types completely corresponds to the clear words in the
New Testament. We need the proper understanding to com-
prehend these types. Some people, when they read the Old
Testament types, such as the ordinances concerning the tab-
ernacle and the offerings in Exodus and Leviticus, feel that
they are insignificant and hard to understand. When I first
began to read the Bible, I felt the same way. Whenever I came
to genealogies, types, and prophecies, I wanted to skip over
them. Today, however, I can say that some of the most precious items in the Bible are the types.

The Old Testament describes the year of jubilee very well.
Leviticus 25 is a long chapter, but it has only two main
points. The first point is that in the year of jubilee all those
who had lost their possession were returned to it. The possession was not returned to its original owner; it was the owner
who was returned to his possession. On the one hand, man
left and lost his possession, but on the other hand, his possession lost him. Did we lose God, or did God lose us? Both are
true; we lost God, and God lost us. As we have seen, the parable of the prodigal son in Luke 15 is an illustration of the
year of jubilee. We are all the real prodigal sons. Today even
kings, presidents, prime ministers, and cabinet officials are
prodigal sons. In this parable, did the son lose his father, or
did the father lose his son? This parable mainly does not
speak of the son's losing the father. In verse 24 the father
said, "This son of mine was dead and lives again; he was lost
and has been found." From this verse we can see that the
father's losing the son is emphasized more than the son's
losing the father. Therefore, in the year of jubilee we mainly
do not have our possession restored to us; rather, we are

returned to our possession. Primarily, God is not restored to us; we are returned to God. The greatest blessing in the year of jubilee is that we are returned to God as our possession. This is the first main point in Leviticus 25.

MAN HAVING REAL FREEDOM
BY ENJOYING GOD AS HIS POSSESSION

The other main point in Leviticus 25 is that we have obtained freedom. Because we were poor, we not only lost God as our possession but also sold ourselves as slaves. Since we sold ourselves, we lost our freedom. However, when the year of jubilee comes, we not only are returned to God as our possession, but we also obtain freedom and are released from the bondage of slavery. Today many people talk about freedom, civil rights, and human rights, but if man does not enjoy God, he cannot have real freedom. When today's politicians speak about freedom, they say nothing about our being returned to God as our possession; therefore, nothing of what they say is of a proper nature. Beginning at least with the French Revolution two hundred years ago, people have been pursuing democracy in order to obtain freedom. However, when people only speak about freedom without being returned to God, the result is that many problems are produced and many evil things are brought in. Who has obtained real freedom? If someone says that he is so free that he can go freely to gamble, he does not realize that he has fallen into the slavery of gambling and is under more bondage than ever. Seventy years ago in China, women and young people had little freedom. They had to rise when they saw their fathers, grandfathers, or uncles come in the room, and they yielded their seats to them politely. Today in America, however, most children do not yield their seats to their father or even to their grandfather; in this sense, they are very free. However, many children in former times had true freedom, while today's children have the wrong freedom, a freedom under the yoke of slavery. In the same principle, the yoke of slavery borne by many women today is worse than before because many women today do not have God. The biblical principle is that we must first be returned to God before we can have freedom. If we want to obtain freedom without being returned to God, the result is that we do not have true freedom.

THE TRUE HUMAN CONDITION—
POOR, CAPTURED, AND OPPRESSED

Man has lost God and is without God because of the fall. Therefore, when the Bible speaks of the year of jubilee, the first thing it teaches is that man must be returned to God. Then when we have God and enjoy Him, we have the real freedom. According to the Old Testament type, when the year of jubilee came, a person who had sold himself into slavery was returned to his own possession and to his own family to be reunited with his relatives, and at the same time he was also released from the yoke of slavery and was no longer a slave. In the New Testament age, in Luke 4, the Lord spoke of the condition of three kinds of people. Verse 18 says, "The Spirit of the Lord is upon Me, because He has anointed Me to announce the gospel to the poor; He has sent Me to proclaim release to the captives, and recovery of sight to the blind, to send away in release those who are oppressed." The three categories of people in this verse are the poor, the captives, and the oppressed. On the one hand, these are three kinds of people, but on the other hand, they are three human conditions. When we lost God, we became poor, and the result of poverty was that we were captured. Then after being captured, we were oppressed. When the year of jubilee comes, however, we obtain freedom and are delivered from poverty, captivity, and oppression.

When I was young, I did not know whether *the poor* denotes those who are poor materially or poor spiritually. Some may say that *poor* denotes being poor in material things, and material poverty symbolizes spiritual poverty. This way of explaining this verse is wrong. The really poor people are not those who have no money. The really poor ones are those who do not have God. We may consider today's millionaires; even though they have much wealth, if the emptiness in the depths of their being cannot be satisfied, are they not poor? To be without God is to be really poor. Material riches mean nothing. Paul said that material matters were like refuse to him. He said, "On account of whom [Christ] I have suffered the loss of all things and count them as refuse that I may gain Christ" (Phil. 3:8). He counted all things as refuse for Christ's sake. The meaning of the word *refuse* is *dog food,* that is, dregs and rubbish that are thrown to the dogs. What Paul means by this is that if a man on earth does not have God, then whatever he enjoys apart from God is like dog food. Only God is man's real food. The Lord Jesus said that He is the bread of life. Apart from Him, everything is dog food or worse than dog food. When the prodigal son in Luke 15 left his father, he left his inheritance. As a result, he had to eat hog food, which may be worse than dog food. There was an abundance of food in his father's house, but he himself was so poor that he had to eat hog food. Please remember that it is not those who do not have money who are poor; rather, it is the people who do not have God who are poor.

Hence, the phrase *announce the gospel to the poor* in Luke 4 actually means to preach the gospel to those who are without God. This corresponds to Ephesians 2:12, which says that formerly we lived in the world, having no hope and being without God. Why did we not have hope? It was because we did not have God. People who live in the world without God do not have hope. Whether kings, queens, or presidents, all are poor because they live in the world without God. We must not misunderstand the Bible. Announcing the gospel to the poor does not refer to preaching the gospel to those who are poor in material things. Otherwise, millionaires, bankers, and presidents would not need the gospel, since they are not poor in material things. The accurate meaning here is that all men, whether rich or poor, honored or despised, need the gospel, and they need to gain God.

Moreover, Luke 4:18 says, "To proclaim release to the captives." America today is the freest country; no one can wrongly capture anyone here. In reality, however, nearly everyone is a captive. The leaders have been captured, and the people have also been captured. Who captured them? According to Acts 26:18, the Lord told Saul of Tarsus that He would send him to the Gentiles "to open their eyes, to turn them from darkness to light and from the authority of Satan to God." Strictly speaking, we have all been captured by Satan. All human beings, regardless of their occupation, gender, or age, are captives of Satan and are under his authority. Apparently, human beings are free, but actually in the whole world no one is free because all are captives under the authority of Satan. First John 5:19 says, "The whole world lies in the evil one." All the people of the world remain passively in the sphere of the evil one's influence, under the evil one's usurpation and manipulation.

The Bible never says that fallen people are the slaves of Satan; rather, it says that fallen people are the slaves of sin and the captives of Satan. Satan has captured us, and sin has enslaved us. Being a captive is much like being a slave, but there are some basic differences. In Romans 7:14 Paul says, "I am fleshy, sold under sin." To be sold under sin means that we have sold ourselves as slaves to sin. However, we are not the captives of sin; we are the captives of Satan and the slaves of sin.

Now we must go further to see what sin is. The common definition is that rape, robbery, sorcery, and fornication are sin. Likewise, extravagant eating, drunkenness, sexual indulgence, and gambling are also sin. Similarly, murder and arson are sin; not honoring one's father and mother is sin; stealing and looting are sin; lying and cheating are sin; and cursing and hating are sin. However, in the intrinsic sense, these are not the real sin. Sin is something intrinsic in man's being; murder and arson are merely the outward, sinful acts that are carried out and manifested. They may be regarded as the results of sin, but they are not sin itself. What, then, is sin? The Chinese followers of Confucius studied this matter carefully. The result of their studies produced the two great and opposing theories of human nature in Confucianism: the theory that human nature is good and the theory that human nature is evil. Advocates of the former asserted that man is born good, while proponents of the latter maintained that man is born evil. However, they did not carry out their research to the extent of knowing the real meaning of sin. In actuality, sin is just Satan. Romans 7 says that sin can dwell

in us (v. 20). Normally we say that a table is placed in a
house; no one would say that a table dwells in a house. Only
living persons can dwell in a house. The fact that sin dwells
in us proves that sin is in us as a living person. Romans 7
also says that the sin which dwells in us has killed us (v. 11).
A table cannot kill, but sin kills. Before sin kills a person, it
oppresses him, forcing him to do what he does not want to do.
Sin is a "gangster" who coerces people to do what they do not
desire to do. Paul said that he did not want to covet, but the
sin that dwelt in him made him unable to control himself. He
said that to will to do good was present with him, but to work
out the good was not, because someone who was stronger
than him dwelt in him. This one not only overcame him but
also killed him. In this way, the Bible reveals that sin is
Satan.

Before Satan entered into man, sin was not embodied;
after Satan came into man, sin was embodied in man. There is
no school of sin to teach people to sin. No parents would teach
their children how to sin, but it is remarkable that as children
grow, they spontaneously commit sins without anyone teaching them. This is because the sin that dwells in them drives
them to commit sins. As a person's will develops, he may feel
that sinning is not good, and he therefore no longer wants to
commit sin. However, the sin within him does not let him go,
and it forces him to do that which he does not want to do. We
can see this particularly in those who smoke opium, drink,
and gamble. When some people do these things, even their
visage appears demonic. They are very clear that if they keep
gambling, they will lose all their money and become poor, but
the addiction within them drives and pressures them to
gamble. An addiction is a lust. Addiction to alcohol, tobacco,
and drugs comes from Satan. Once a person has become
addicted to gambling, he cannot stop himself from gambling,
and once someone has become addicted to alcohol, he cannot
stop himself from drinking. When his addiction to alcohol
makes its demand, he must have a drink, and when the addiction to gambling rises up, he must gamble. There are no
exceptions to this pattern. After the addiction abates and a
person comes to his senses, he regrets what he has done. He

regrets that he has shamed his parents, wife, and children. Then he may call upon heaven and earth to witness his oath that he will never do it again. However, only a few hours later when the addiction returns, he is powerless against it.

Thus, there is a sinning factor, an addiction to sinning within man. This factor, this addiction, is Satan himself, and man is his captive. He has captured man and dwells in him as the inciting sin. First Satan captured us; then he came to dwell in us as the inciter, the instigator, of our sins. The result is that he has become our illegal master, and we have become his captives to the extent that we are unable to do good and can only commit sins. In the Bible, Satan is also called Beelzebul. According to the original language of the Bible, Beelzebul means *the lord of the dunghill,* from the name meaning *the lord of flies.* The top of a dunghill is covered with flies. As the lord of the dunghill, Satan specializes in leading flies to feed on dung; hence, he is also the lord of flies. Since he is the lord of flies, all sinners are like flies that follow Satan to "feed on dung." They go wherever there is a stench, following Beelzebul to feast on dung. Even upper-class people are like flies. Beelzebul can disguise himself with a high-class appearance so that all the "flies" following him appear to be of a high class. Such persons hold dancing parties in upper-class places, but such places are merely cultured "dunghills." These people dress nicely and are very cultured, and when they dance they seem elegant. In actuality, however, they are "eating dung."

All the descendants of Adam are the captives of Satan; everyone has been captured by him. After he captured us, he entered into us as Beelzebul, the lord of flies, and began leading us about to commit sins. Deep in his heart, no one wants to sin, but when a person becomes addicted and is stirred up by Beelzebul, he has to follow, allowing himself to be led around "by the nose." Afterward he regrets it and may say, "I am so stupid; what was I doing? Why did I have to do that?" Although deep in his heart no one wants to sin, eventually everyone sins. No one has control over himself, and everyone has become a slave of sin. This is why the Lord Jesus said, "Everyone who commits sin is a slave of sin" (John 8:34).

One who becomes angry at someone and then can immediately get over his anger may be considered to be a sage and a virtuous man. Logically, as saved ones, the saints, we should surpass the sages and virtuous ones, but can we quickly get over our anger? It is not easy to come back to the Lord after we get angry. Perhaps a person may be one who has learned the lessons well and is able to come back to the Lord and calm his anger. However, after such a one leaves the Lord's presence, his anger may return again when he sees the offending person. Wood and stones do not become angry, but no human being can avoid getting angry; only dead people do not get angry. All these problems are due to the fact that man is under bondage and has no freedom. The sin within us is a real controlling power. In Romans 7:24 Paul said, "Wretched man that I am! Who will deliver me from the body of this death?" How we thank God for Romans 8:2, which says that in Christ the law of the Spirit of life frees us from the law of sin and of death! We thank the Lord for His mercy. Many can testify that when they get angry, they can get over it very quickly, and the anger does not come back. This is because the law of the Spirit of life frees us from the bondage of sin!

BEING RELEASED AND HAVING REAL FREEDOM
ONLY BY ENJOYING GOD AS THE LIFE-GIVING SPIRIT

In Luke 4:18-19 the Lord Jesus quoted the words of the prophet Isaiah, saying, "The Spirit of the Lord is upon Me, because He has anointed Me to announce the gospel to the poor; He has sent Me to proclaim release to the captives, and recovery of sight to the blind, to send away in release those who are oppressed, to proclaim the acceptable year of the Lord, the year of jubilee." As we have seen, to announce the gospel to the poor is to preach the gospel to those who have lost God, and *those who are oppressed* refers to those in slavery. We should not think that the year of jubilee came to free us only on the day we were saved. Actually, the entire age of the New Testament is the age of the jubilee. We have our entire Christian life in the jubilee, living a life of liberty, release, and freedom from bondage.

Announcing the gospel to the poor, proclaiming release to the captives, and sending away in release those who are oppressed are the freedoms of the jubilee. These are the blessings of the jubilee, the blessings of the gospel. The blessings of the gospel are the return to God and the gaining of God as our possession. Once we enjoy God as our possession, we are free. Only those who enjoy God do not commit sin and are really free. John 8:36 says, "If therefore the Son sets you free, you shall be free indeed." If we want to be free, if we do not want to commit sin, then we must obtain the Son of God and enjoy Him. The Son of God today is the life-giving Spirit. This life-giving Spirit is the Spirit of life, who is in us as the law of the Spirit of life. Therefore, the law of the Spirit of life is just the Lord Himself, who passed through death and resurrection to become the life-giving Spirit, the Spirit of life. Every life has a law, so the Spirit of life also has a law. The law of the Spirit of life releases us from the law of sin. We enjoy the freedom of the jubilee not only at the moment we believe in the Lord, but beginning from that day we should enjoy this freedom all our life and for eternity. This freedom comes from our enjoyment of God. He has become our possession for our enjoyment, and when we enjoy Him, we obtain freedom. This is how we have the real freedom and are no longer in bondage. However, if we do not enjoy God sufficiently, we will still be in bondage in many things.

In conclusion, the year of jubilee is for us to be returned to God as our possession and as our enjoyment so that we may become free and be released from all oppression. Thus, we are returned to God from the authority of Satan and are freed from the slavery of sin. Hence, it is useless to struggle and strive. The only effective way for us is to believe the gospel and enjoy God. Some may say, "I will go home and make up my mind not to be angry or lose my temper again," but whereas one can make up his mind to do good, he does not have the power to perform the good. Making up our mind will not work; we must enjoy the Lord. We must learn to contact this true and living Lord to enjoy Him. In this way, He becomes our release within us and our freedom. As a result, we have not only our possession but also our freedom.

Chapter Four

THE LIVING OF THE JUBILEE

Scripture Reading: Lev. 25:10-12; Psa. 90:9-10; 73:14-17, 25; Eccl. 1:2-3; Rom. 8:19-21; Matt. 11:28; Phil. 4:6-7, 9; 1 Cor. 5:8; Eph. 3:8; Phil. 1:19; 2 Cor. 12:9; 13:14

RECOVERING OUR LOST PORTION—
LIVING THE LIFE OF THE JUBILEE
IN THE AGE OF THE JUBILEE

In the first chapter, we saw that the Lord has come to bring in the New Testament age as the age of the jubilee. In the second chapter we saw that the possession of the jubilee is God Himself. God has become our inheritance, the portion of our cup, and our eternal dwelling place in all generations. Since God is our inheritance, our enjoyment should be God. In the third chapter we saw the freedom of the jubilee. Freedom means release, to be freed from all bondage, all heavy burden, all oppression, and all enslavement. Paul said that all things were lawful to him, but he would not be brought under the power of anything to be its slave (1 Cor. 6:12). Everything in our life can be a bondage to us, and we can be slaves under any matter. To pursue education is to be enslaved, and to not pursue education is also to be enslaved. The poor are ruled by poverty, while the rich are ruled by money; the Chinese expression for *miser* refers to one who is a slave of money. The jubilee is a matter of possession and also of freedom. The jubilee is to return those who are poor and who have lost God back to God as their possession, and it is also to proclaim release.

In the holy year, the year of jubilee, freedom is proclaimed to all the people. Today in the age of democracy people greatly promote freedom, but the result is that they have very little freedom. Based on nearly sixty years of observation, I have found that people are much more free when they do not pursue outward freedom. We may illustrate this with political freedom. Sixty years ago, there was a certain amount of political freedom in China. No one would interfere with others, taxation was simple, and people could freely travel without permits. Today, however, after much pursuit of freedom, traveling is very troublesome, and there are many restrictions. People continually talk about liberty and seek for freedom, but eventually they are bound and restricted in every way. Wherever we go on the earth, there are bondage and restrictions. People often use doves to symbolize liberty. "Liberty doves" are released during celebrations, but after the doves are released, they never return. In the same manner, once freedom is "released," it "flies away." If we do not pursue freedom, we may enjoy some amount of freedom, but the more we talk about freedom, the more we lose it. Many people consider that America is free, but the freedom in America is an unrestrained freedom. There is little real freedom here. American society is full of entertainment, crime, dancing, gambling, and other matters. All these are very strong bondage. Americans fall into bondage because they are too free. As a result of this kind of freedom, they fall into indulgence and are enslaved. The Lord's salvation causes us to have real freedom. The Lord Jesus said, "If therefore the Son sets you free, you shall be free indeed" (John 8:36). We can only enjoy real freedom when we have Christ, the Son of God.

THE REAL CONDITION OF HUMAN LIFE BEING VANITY

Now we will consider the living of the jubilee. The jubilee is not a mere doctrine or simply a declaration; the jubilee is a kind of living. When the year of jubilee came and the trumpet sounded, release was proclaimed throughout the land. This ushered in a practical living, on the one hand, of enjoying the life of rich possession, and on the other hand, of enjoying freedom. The jubilee is a type in the Old Testament, but in the New Testament it is fulfilled in all those who believe in the Lord. However, if we do not know the real condition of human life, we do not know how much we need the jubilee.

Every person is like a glass filled with the wrong content. For the glass to contain the right drink, it must be emptied; to know our real condition is to be emptied. For this reason we will present a clear picture from the Bible of the real condition of human life. If we see this picture, we will not be deceived about human life.

Hymns, #1080, which was written based on Ecclesiastes, depicts the actual condition of human life. The real condition of life is neither good fortune nor misfortune. Actually, both good fortune and misfortune are useless. The true condition of human life can be summed up in one word, vanity. The wise king Solomon said that a man has no advantage in all his work which he does under the sun, and a generation goes and another generation comes, yet there is no remembrance of those who were before; hence, all is vanity of vanities (Eccl. 1:2-11). All things of the human life are vanity, like pursuing after shadows and chasing after wind; they are fleeting and short-lived.

Psalm 90:1 says, "O Lord, You have been our dwelling place / In all generations." This declaration is the proclamation of the jubilee, but verse 9 says, "For all our days have passed away in Your overflowing wrath; / We bring our years to an end as with a sigh." These words thoroughly portray the real condition of human life. There is nothing much worth singing about in the entire life of a man. When Moses wrote this psalm, he was over eighty years old, perhaps almost one hundred twenty years old. Having had the experience of human life, he said that we bring all the years of our life to an end as with a sigh. Little children do not know about human life, so they do not sigh. However, old men are always sighing; they sigh from morning until evening. They sigh when they think about themselves, they sigh when they think about their children and grandchildren, and they sigh when they think about their relatives and friends. There is nothing that does not make them sigh. Even when they sing, they cannot sing for too long, because eventually their song becomes a dirge or a lamentation. The days of man's entire life are nothing but a sigh. Verse 10 goes on to say, "The days of our years are in sum seventy years, / Or, if because of strength, eighty years; / But their pride is labor and sorrow, / For it is soon gone, and we fly away." This is a word of experience spoken by Moses as an old man. His description of human life is thorough. A person may live to the age of eighty years due to his strength, but all that he can boast of is nothing but labor and sorrow, for his life is soon gone and he flies away. Even though I am also eighty years old, I hope to live for forty more years, because I enjoy the Lord and I have hope. If one lives to the age of eighty without the Lord, then the phrase *labor and sorrow..it is soon gone, and we fly away* is a description and a true portrait of the real condition of his human life. The Bible is the only book that speaks the truth; every philosophy and "ism" is deceiving. The Bible says that the real condition of human life is only "labor and sorrow..it is soon gone, and we fly away." Ecclesiastes 1:2 says, "Vanity of vanities; all is vanity." In Hebrew, *vanity of vanities* means *emptiness of emptiness.* Solomon's words fully agree with the words of Moses. Moses said, "It is soon gone, and we fly away," whereas Solomon said, "All is vanity and a chasing after wind" (v. 14).

Psalm 73 was written by a seeker of God. In verse 14 the seeker said, "For I have been plagued all day long / And chastened every morning." Before they are enlightened by the Lord, many believers are like this psalmist. It seems to them that even though they are seeking the Lord and loving Him, they end up receiving plagues and chastisements. Even though the psalmist loved the Lord out of a pure heart, everything was an affliction to him. Consequently he could only say that he had been plagued all day long and chastened every morning. Then he went on to say, "When I considered this in order to understand it, / It was troublesome in my sight, / Until I went into the sanctuary of God; / Then I perceived their end" (vv. 16-17). Once he went into the sanctuary, received the enlightenment, and carefully considered this matter, he understood. Having understood, he went on to say, "Whom do I have in heaven but You? / And besides You there is nothing I desire on earth" (v. 25). In this way, he was led from vanity into reality, which is just God Himself. Because he passed through vanity, the psalmist, who was rich in experience, realized the real situation. It is as if he was saying, "Since everything under the sun is vanity, why should I pursue them? To do so makes me a fool. Now that I have woken up to reality, I do not want any of these things. What I want is the God who fills heaven and earth. Having Him, I do not pursue anyone else in heaven, and having Him, I do not desire anyone else on earth."

It is not easy for many Christians to turn in this way. This is because when man thinks of God, the fear of God is aroused in him, and when he begins to fear God, he comes under the philosophy that God will be kind to him and that the more he fears God, the more prosperous he will become, the healthier he will be, the more children and grandchildren he will have, and the more he will have good fortune and not misfortune. When I was small, I often heard my mother say, "Giving birth to a son lasts a moment, but fearing for a son lasts a lifetime." I have experienced the truth of this word. Once a son is born, his parents are afraid that he may not survive. They are afraid that he may not eat or drink well or that he may catch a cold and become sick. After this, they are afraid that he may not get into a good elementary school, junior high school, or high school, and once he gets into a good school, they are afraid that he may not pass the entrance examination to get into a good university. After he is admitted to a good university, the parents are afraid that he may not pass the English language examination to be able to go to America, and after he passes the examination, they are afraid that he may not be able to get into a good graduate school. Furthermore, they are afraid that he may misbehave himself with young friends or marry the wrong wife. Such fears are endless. Therefore, human life is nothing but labor and sorrow and will be soon gone. There is no genuine good fortune.

Job is a long book of forty-two chapters. Some readers do not grasp the significance of this book, and they lose interest when they read it. The characters in Job seem to argue the whole time. At first, Job's three friends argue with Job; later, Elihu joins in, and finally, even God Himself joins in. In recent years, however, I have begun to have more appreciation of the book of Job. Although this book is of considerable length with forty-two chapters, it deals with only one issue. Job was originally a man blessed with possessions and children, but suddenly calamities came one after another—his livestock was stolen, his possessions were burnt, and his children were killed in an unnatural way. Natural disasters and man-made calamities came one after the other, causing Job to end up with nothing. Not only so, but Job's wife troubled him. She could not comfort Job even a little; on the contrary, she provoked him, saying in effect, "See, you fear God, yet what do you end up with?" God took everything away from Job and left him with only a mocker. When a person is smitten repeatedly to the extent that everything he has is gone, he truly needs sympathy from others, but all those who could comfort him had died. Of all the sufferings of Job, the most severe was the mocking from his wife. This caused Job to suffer exceedingly. It seemed that God had been extremely cruel. Nonetheless, after passing through these trials, Job gained God. He was able to say, "Jehovah gives and Jehovah takes away; / Blessed be the name of Jehovah" (1:21). Had Job not encountered this stripping and suffering, his experience and enjoyment of God could not have been as great.

THE SECRET OF A CHRISTIAN'S ENJOYMENT OF REST BEING GAINING GOD AS HIS ENJOYMENT

The book of James in the New Testament says that we need to consider the experience of Job and remember how he endured (5:11). Both James and Peter acknowledge that our Christian life is altogether a life of trials (1:2; 1 Pet. 4:12). God did not promise that we Christians will have everything to our satisfaction on earth. Perhaps after some hear this word, they will say, "Are you not contradicting yourself? Didn't you tell us that the jubilee means that all things are to our satisfaction?" Yes, everything is to our satisfaction but not the things themselves; rather, our satisfaction is in God. If we do not have God, nothing is to our satisfaction. If we have God, everything is to our satisfaction. Whether or not something is to our satisfaction does not depend on the environment; it depends on whether or not God is there. Without God, even if all things go smoothly, they are not to our satisfaction. But once we have

God, even if things do not go smoothly, they are still to our satisfaction.

What Job encountered in his life was very difficult, but he was still satisfied, and he could still worship and praise. It seems that he was saying, "Being given something and having something taken away are the same. There is no difference between many possessions being given to me and my possessions being taken away from me. It does not matter whether Jehovah gives or Jehovah takes away; to me, they are the same." This is not easy to experience. Paul said, "I know also how to be abased, and I know how to abound" (Phil. 4:12). It did not matter to Paul whether he was poor or rich or whether he was lacking or abounding. Therefore, he could say, "In nothing be anxious" (v. 6). If we only read verse 6, we may think that Paul was in a good situation. In reality though, it was not so, because at that time he was in prison. Moreover, according to the context, he did not receive a rich supply during his imprisonment. The churches had received his nurturing, but they did not supply him adequately. Only the church in Philippi took care of him. This is why he said, "I know also how to be abased, and I know how to abound...I am able to do all things in Him who empowers me" (vv. 12-13). He was very qualified to tell us to be anxious in nothing. Even though he was in a poor circumstance in his imprisonment and did not receive a rich supply at that time, he was able to exhort the saints to be anxious in nothing. He could be anxious in nothing because he made known all his requests to God; thus, the peace of God, which surpasses every man's understanding, guarded his heart and his thoughts in Christ Jesus (v. 7). In this way, he enjoyed the presence of the God of peace. Therefore, only when we have God, do we have real peace. Even if there is no peace in our environment, if we have God, we have peace.

MAN LOSING THE ORDAINED BLESSING WHEN HE LOSES GOD

Man was created for God, and God is man's blessing. However, because man sinned and became fallen, he lost God and thus his blessing. Hence, man's whole life became empty. Man not only lost God in his fall, but he also fell into bondage. We may say that human history of six thousand years is a history of losing God and being in bondage. Because man does not have God, he struggles to obtain enjoyment. The result of man's struggle and strife is that he falls into all kinds of bondage. Everything in human life is a bondage. Even our relatives become a bondage to us: our parents, children, spouse, and siblings are all a bondage. This is why the Lord Jesus said that if we do not love Him above our father or mother, sons or daughters, brothers or sisters, and husband or wife, we are not worthy to be His disciples (Matt. 10:37-38). This means that if our inward being is occupied by any person or thing, the Lord has no ground in us. Since man was created by God, he should be fully occupied by God within. However, this does not mean that we should not take care of our children and parents or that we should not care for our brothers or sisters and wife or husband. What this means is that all the room in our being must be given to the Lord. When the Lord has gained the ground in us, we will be secure. When I was a small child, I saw big sailboats and wondered why their masts were so tall. I thought that the tall mast was only for hanging the sail in order to catch the wind. Later, some sailors told me that the mast is not only for hanging the sail but also for stabilizing the boat. A sailboat with a tall mast cannot be easily capsized. After I was saved, I realized how this is altogether true in our experience. Without the Lord, we are like a sailboat without a mast, having no stability, so that we drift aimlessly. If we do not have the Lord as our "mast," the "boat" of our human life is unstable and can be easily overturned. Our human life can be capsized if it is empty within. If a glass is filled to the brim, impure things cannot get in. In the same way, if we are filled with the Lord, things that are not of the Lord cannot come in.

Christians in general have a wrong concept, and some preachers even lead them into this wrong concept. They think that although there are sufferings in their human life, when they believe in Jesus, they will have peace in their environment. They consider that although life is full of sufferings and adversities, Jesus, who is full of compassion, will outwardly rescue them from their sufferings when they believe in Him.

This is not the biblical concept. Actually, what the gospel says is that we as fallen ones have all kinds of suffering because we have lost God and do not have Him within. Even the outward blessings enjoyed by fallen man are a suffering. After man's fall, there is no blessing; rather, everything is a suffering. Moreover, not only does fallen man not have the Lord, but he also sins against Him. Therefore, he needs to repent, confess his sins, turn to the Lord, and let Him come into him to be his life and blessing. This is the message of the gospel.

Of course, after receiving the Lord, some have experienced a turning point in their broken marriage, others have been cured of a critical illness, and still others have experienced an improvement in their difficult situations. I have seen many such cases, but it is not always so. After receiving the Lord, some who were gravely ill prayed continually to the Lord for healing, yet the Lord never healed them. Healing does not depend on us; it depends on Him. What the gospel stresses is not that our sickness will be healed but that we need to receive the Lord and allow Him to come into us to be our life and our blessing. Sometimes we may call upon the Lord concerning our circumstances, but He may or may not answer our call. Whether or not He answers depends wholly on Him. The Bible does not say that all those who believe in Jesus will have their sickness healed. Timothy, who was Paul's dearest young co-worker and whom Paul called his genuine child, had a stomach ailment. Nevertheless, even though Paul had performed many signs and wonders and had healed many diseases (Acts 19:11-12), he told his spiritual son, his beloved Timothy, to "no longer drink water only, but use a little wine for the sake of your stomach and your frequent illnesses" (1 Tim. 5:23). Even Paul himself had a thorn in his flesh (2 Cor. 12:7). Many Bible interpreters say that this thorn was a sickness in his body, most likely a problem with his eyes. This thorn remained with Paul all the time, causing him to suffer. He said, "Concerning this I entreated the Lord three times that it might depart from me" (v. 8). However, the Lord seemed to say, "Paul, do not ask this anymore. I will not answer your prayer. I will not remove the thorn from you. Rather, it will constantly remain with you. Nevertheless, My grace is sufficient for you." A number of people had been healed of their diseases simply by means of handkerchiefs or aprons carried away from Paul's body. Yet, when he had a thorn in his flesh that caused him to suffer, he had no way to remove it. Furthermore, he was imprisoned late in life. In his first imprisonment, he appealed to Caesar and was released through Caesar's arbitration, but he was imprisoned a second time during Caesar's persecution of the Christians and was killed soon afterwards. This was Paul's experience before the Lord.

EXPERIENCING GOD IN TRIALS

As fallen ones, we may have the fallen natural concept that if we fear God, serve Him, love Him, and follow Him, we will prosper in everything; the unhealthy will become healthy and the foolish will become wise. However, God has not promised this. *Hymns,* #720 was written by an experienced Christian. Verse 1 and the chorus say,

God hath not promised skies always blue,
Flower-strewn pathways all our lives through;
God hath not promised sun without rain,
Joy without sorrow, peace without pain.

But God hath promised strength for the day,
Rest for the labor, light for the way,
Grace for the trials, help from above,
Unfailing sympathy, undying love.

Many times, God has placed those who love Him into trials and sufferings that they may experience more of Him. When everything is calm and peaceful, we seldom think of enjoying God and know very little about experiencing the Lord. Only when we fall into sufferings can we be humbled to trust the Lord wholeheartedly, call on Him, and enjoy Him.

This is why man often needs to be put into a situation by God to be stripped by Him. God may strip him of his health, take away his children, or remove the thing he loves most. This is a time of "weaning." A small child is comfortable, warm, and satisfied in his mother's bosom, but sooner or later he has to be weaned. A child suffers great sorrow during the weaning period. Very often, God "weans" us by taking away our outward blessings. Our health may leave us, we may lose our house, or our better children may die while the naughty ones remain. I have seen this happen. God may not take anything at first, but once He does, He only takes the best. He does not take the foolish children—He leaves them with us to make trouble—but He may take those who are clever, capable, and comforting. God wants to see whether we care for Him or for our children. Only God is not a suffering to us. Everything else, whatever we love, is a suffering to us. If we buy a car and love it, that car burdens us and damages us. When we buy a good house, that house puts us under bondage and brings pain to us. Even when we buy good clothes, they become a limitation to us. Whatever man loves is what damages him, but if we love God, God will not damage us. Apparently, it seems that God hurts us by taking away what we love and what, apparently, should not be taken away. Actually, He takes away what we love because we love that thing more than God. Abraham was tested by God. One day, God told Abraham to offer his son up to Him. Yet, when Abraham began to offer up his son, God said in effect, "This is good enough; you can keep him." God no longer wanted him to offer his son. God does the same to us. If we can give all we have to God, He can also give it back to us. Therefore, we have to change our concept.

THE LIVING OF THE JUBILEE BEING A LIVING OF FULLY ENJOYING GOD

What is the living of the jubilee? The living of the jubilee is a life in which we take God instead of other things as our enjoyment and enjoy only God Himself in every situation. This is not to say that we should not study. On the contrary, we should study diligently. Neither does it mean that we should not work; we should work dutifully. Likewise, it does not mean that we should not be proper parents raising our children; rather, we should properly fulfill our responsibilities as parents. However, all these are just our living, our outward human life, which is not crucial. What is crucial is that the inward, primary factor of our human life is right. If our inward, primary factor is not right, our outward living will not be right. This primary factor is nothing other than God Himself. We must let God Himself be the primary factor within us. Only then will we know how to deal with our children, how to honor our parents, how to study, and how to work. If this primary factor directs us within, everything will simply be a duty to us, not a burden or hardship. However, if we are not directed by this primary factor, everything will become a weight and a suffering. In the end, we will become captives and even sell ourselves as slaves.

For us to live on earth today, we need to have a car for transportation and a house for lodging. We need clothing, food, and marriage. All these are necessities. Children should study diligently, be educated, finish college, and work hard. However, all these are just the duties of our human life; they should not become an encumbrance or a bondage to enslave us. However, if we do not have God as our primary factor within, we cannot avoid being under the bondage of these persons, things, and matters. We should be encouraged to get married, but we must not turn marriage into an encumbrance. When choosing a partner for marriage, our attention should not be focused on marriage, as an encumbering burden, but on God. We should also be encouraged to study, but studying should be an obligation and not a burden to us. As we are fulfilling our duty, we must have the Lord within. Often people ask me how they should choose a partner for marriage. Fifty years ago, I used to answer in many ways, but today I do not like to give suggestions. If one does not have the Lord, whomever he chooses is wrong. Even if everything seems to be right at the time of his choosing, once he is married, he may feel that he chose the wrong person.

The Christian life should be a life of fully enjoying the Lord. When we enjoy the Lord fully, He becomes our jubilee; that is, He becomes our inheritance and liberty. Not only so, the Lord also becomes our living. In such a living, we love Him to the uttermost and let Him be the Lord. Then He becomes the primary factor and center in us to lead us and govern us. In this way, when we pass through things, we will not be tormented, enslaved, or dominated by them. Instead, we will be free. I hope we can understand this word. By the Lord's mercy today I have reached the age of eighty. I have passed through all the sweetness and bitterness of life, and I have thirty to forty children and grandchildren. Therefore, I have many troubles and many cares. Without the Lord as my primary factor and center within, I would suffer considerably. However, because the Lord is in me, I do not have any burden or hardship. Moreover, I do not put any hope in my children, my grandchildren, or my great grandchildren because I know that with hope there is disappointment. One who does not hope will not be disappointed, but the more one hopes, the more he is disappointed. Perhaps some will say, "Since this is the case, is there any meaning to human life? Let us give up." Those who study history see the extent of the confusion among people in the world and often say that human life is hopeless. However, we may give up, but God will never give up. We can feel meaningless, but God does not. Although He has been dealing with mankind for six thousand years, He is not through. God will not give up; He is still waiting, and with Him a thousand years are like one day. God is waiting to gain us as those who have been chosen by Him, and He will work to the extent that His chosen ones on earth do not desire anything other than Him and are for nothing besides Him.

For our existence we cannot avoid having a family and a married life. We are also obligated to obtain an education and work at a job. However, all these are not our burdens; on the contrary, they are working for us that we may be perfected to enjoy the Lord even more. This is the living of the jubilee. A Christian's life of jubilee should be a life of fully enjoying the Lord, a life that is full of joy and praises. If we cannot rejoice and praise, it proves that we are not living a normal life of the jubilee. This is why 1 Thessalonians 5:18 says, "In everything give thanks." This is to give thanks not only in things that are successful but in all things.

The Lord came that He might save us and dispense Himself into us. If our heart is set on anything other than the Lord, that thing, whether good or bad, becomes a suffering to us. If our heart is set on our children, husband, or wife, the result is a suffering. If our heart is set on our education, business, house, or land, the outcome is misery. If our heart is set on any person, thing, or matter other than the Lord, the end is wretchedness. The unbelievers do not have the Lord; they have not received the Lord as their salvation. Hence, they can only set their heart on persons, things, and matters. However, since we have been saved and have the Lord as our center, we should set our heart on Him. When the Lord comes, He is our salvation to deliver us from sufferings. All sufferings come from the persons, things, and matters outside of the Lord. To those who are without the Lord, everything is a suffering. Whether bad things or good things, whether poverty or riches, whether being educated or uneducated, all are sufferings. However, when we have the Lord, He saves us from all these sufferings. If we take the Lord as our center, we can enjoy Him as our life of jubilee.

The living of the jubilee is a living in the enjoyment of Christ. The Lord is sovereign in everything. Everything we have is in the Lord's sovereign hand and whatever He arranges for us cannot be wrong. In my life of following the Lord for sixty years, I can truly testify that where we go or where we stay is entirely not in our hands but in His hands. We may think that we are what we are today because of our endeavoring and struggling, but we must realize that without the Lord's sovereign arrangement, no matter how much we struggled and endeavored, we could not be what we are. Everything is under His sovereignty. Therefore, we should empty ourselves of everything and tell the Lord, "Fill me, gain me, and possess me. Lord, no matter what the outward situation is, I just want to enjoy You. If I am healthy, I thank You. If I am not healthy, I also thank You. If I have children, I thank You, and if I am childless, I also thank You." In this way, poverty or wealth and peace or danger are all the same to us. That is why Paul said that "as always, even now Christ will be magnified in my body, whether through life or through death" (Phil. 1:20b). For us to live is Christ, and whether we live or die, He is magnified in us all the time. In this way, we enjoy God and live the life of the jubilee. May the Lord have mercy upon us that we all may see this and learn to enjoy the Lord to such an extent.